ISBN 978-1-332-75211-9
PIBN 10436530

1 MONTH OF FREE READING

at

www.ForgottenBooks.com

By purchasing this book you are eligible for one month membership to ForgottenBooks.com, giving you unlimited access to our entire collection of over 700,000 titles via our web site and mobile apps.

To claim your free month visit: www.forgottenbooks.com/free436530

English
Français
Deutsche
Italiano
Español
Português

www.forgottenbooks.com

Mythology Photography **Fiction**
Fishing Christianity **Art** Cooking
Essays Buddhism Freemasonry
Medicine **Biology** Music **Ancient**
Egypt Evolution Carpentry Physics
Dance Geology **Mathematics** Fitness
Shakespeare **Folklore** Yoga Marketing
Confidence Immortality Biographies
Poetry **Psychology** Witchcraft
Electronics Chemistry History **Law**
Accounting **Philosophy** Anthropology
Alchemy Drama Quantum Mechanics
Atheism Sexual Health **Ancient History**
Entrepreneurship Languages Sport
Paleontology Needlework Islam
Metaphysics Investment Archaeology
Parenting Statistics Criminology
Motivational

SHORTHAND
WITHOUT A TEACHER

A COMPLETE COURSE AT HOME

The Pitman-Graham System
Universally Used

SELF-EXPLANATORY

THE CHRISTIAN HERALD

BIBLE HOUSE ·   NEW YORK CITY

THE QUINN & BODEN CO. PRESS
RAHWAY, N. J.

© CI. A 293777

INTRODUCTION

WITHIN the last few years many of the leading educators in our colleges and universities have begun to think so highly of Shorthand that they have already added correspondence courses to their personal methods of teaching. Dr. W. D. Harper, formerly President of the University of Chicago and one of the most conservative educators of his time, wrote ·

" Better opportunity exists in work done by correspondence, for a larger and broader preparation, than is afforded in most cases by actual class-room work. The student makes the recitations to suit himself. He has to recite on all the lessons, whereas, in ordinary recitations in resident courses, the student recites on only about one-thirtieth of the amount covered by the three months' course. Furthermore, it is safe to make the statement that the work done by correspondence is equal to the work done in class; and I go even further and say that there is a larger proportion of high-grade work done by correspondence than in class-rooms."

A STEPPING STONE TO SUCCESS

To the ambitious young man or woman, there is no business or profession that offers so many inducements and yet is so easily acquired as Shorthand. To the person of average intelligence, it will be found extremely fascinating, as well as lucrative. The field for Shorthand work is constantly broadening. Expert Shorthand writers of both sexes, in reporting and commercial lines, are in increasing demand and their emoluments are received sooner than in any other profession.

While a college or high-school education is desirable, it is not essential to success in Shorthand. Daniel B. Lloyd, who is one of the fastest writers in the United States Senate, had few educational advantages. His schooling was received when he was between eight and thirteen, in a little school in Maryland. .

Hon. George Bruce Cortelyou owes much of his phenomenal success to his thorough knowledge of Shorthand. From school teaching, his Shorthand helped him through various minor positions until he finally reached the highest appointive office in the land. In Mr. William Loeb Jr.'s case, Shorthand was also the chief factor in his success.

The National Association of Shorthand Writers established the following rates which are recognized in the various State capitals and many of the large cities for Shorthand reporting work. $10. a day for taking notes and twenty-five cents a folio for the transcript. If copies are furnished to both sides in a lawsuit the transcript fee is doubled. Few professions can offer such alluring inducements as Shorthand affords.

The chances for the Shorthand writer in business and commerce are just as promising as in reporting, law and politics. Many of our leading merchant princes, railroad magnates and financiers state that their success in business life was due to their knowledge of Shorthand. The energetic young man or woman who obtains a position as Shorthand secretary in a railroad office, wholesale house or business concern, has the best opportunity in the world. The Shorthand secretary, through his close and intimate relations with the heads, gets a more thorough and practical knowledge of every detail of the business than could be gotten in any other way. With this knowledge at his command, he can make himself of incalculable value to the concern.

We can confidently assert, that there is no other study to compare with Shorthand as a stepping stone to business success.

THE STANDARD SYSTEM

In taking up the study of Shorthand, the student should be sure to select a system that is in general use. This is of the utmost importance if he wishes his study to be of practical value. In applying for a position, one of the first questions asked is, "What system do you write?" If you have learned a nondescript system, you stand a very poor chance of getting the position. Should you decide to take up the study of Shorthand, *take only the best*.

Pitman-Graham is recognized the world over as the Standard. The world's record for speed is held by a writer of this system. The Standard Pitmanic basis as taught here is written by every member of the reporting staff of the United States Senate and House of Representatives and by 95 per cent of all American and English court stenographers. Over 98 per cent of the successful stenographers in the United States write this system.

METHOD OF INSTRUCTION

Our method of Shorthand instruction is simple, comprehensive and practical, making the lessons easier for the pupil to learn than by any other method yet devised. It is not necessary for the student to give up his position while studying Shorthand. One or two hours a day, morning or evening, whichever is convenient, will be quite sufficient.

The pupil is given practical work from the start. By easy stages, he is taught the alphabet, vowels, joining characters, formation of words sentences, phrases, etc., and given abundant dictation. Every lesson has its exercises to be worked out by the student. From the very start, the lessons are delightfully interesting and so clearly put that the student finds no difficulty in understanding them. The student may advance just as quickly as his time and opportunity will permit. It is to the pupil's advantage, however to *be regular with his lessons.*

STANDARD SHORTHAND

A Word to the Pupil

AT the beginning of this Course, we wish to inspire you with the fullest confidence in your own ability to comprehend every lesson to be set before you. All we ask of you is: 1. A regular study period of one and a half hours each day—you can fix the hours to suit yourself—till you reach the stage of dictation. 2. Work with the regular ruled paper supplied with this Course and a medium soft pencil. 3. Copy out the lessons set for you, repeating aloud the signs as you write them and always filling out the line with the signs. Do not stop with writing each sign once or twice, but fill out the line. 4. When you have finished the lesson, begin again, always filling the line and repeating the names of the signs as you write them. Do this for the full period of one and a half hours. 5. Remember that if you attended shorthand classes under our care, you would be expected to work for a much longer period of study, without cessation.

If you do this faithfully, always reading the lesson first, so as to catch the meaning of it, you will have no difficulty whatsoever. Do not anticipate by beginning on lessons further ahead. Stick to the lesson before you in the regular order. There are two lessons for each week. We would advise that at the end of each week, you should devote the last half hour to a review of that week's lessons, which you will find very helpful in refreshing your memory.

There is no secret or mystery about shorthand. You will find it quite simple and plain throughout, and if you follow the instructions, you will be able at the end of the Course to take correspondence dictation with a considerable amount of satisfaction.

LESSON I

The Phonetic Alphabet

ALL exercises should be written on ruled paper, preferably double-lined, which will enable the pupil to keep his letters of a uniform size. A fine steel pen or a soft pencil should be used. Too great care cannot be given to the formation of the shorthand signs. Make each character one-sixth of an inch long and as nearly like the copy as possible. All light lines should be very light and the heavy ones just a shade darker than the light ones and gradually tapering toward the ends. Use the utmost care in writing, in order that you may acquire a neat as well as a correct style. Don't try for speed; that only comes with familiarity with the characters. Write and rewrite the consonants *over and over again, repeating the names aloud* until you are familiar with each sign and its sound.

The consonants are *all written downward* with the exception of Ray, El and Hay. Ish, Zhee and El are written *both upward and downward*, as may be convenient. A greater slant should be given to Ray and Hay than to Chay and Jay. Write *twenty times* until thoroughly committed to memory:

Pee Bee Tee Dee Chay Jay Kay Gay Ef Vee Ith Thee Ess Zee Ish Zhee

El Lay Ar Ray Em En Ing Way Way Way Yay Yay Yay Hay Iss

After you are able to make a good copy of the letters, fill several pages with them, writing them at least *twenty times*. Then practice writing them in irregular order: El, Chay, Zee, Hay, Em, etc. It should be remembered that all these letters must be called by the names given above. For instance, Gay should be pronounced as it is spelled and not Jee. Each letter represents a definite phonetic sound and it is very important that these should be learned and *pronounced ¢orrectly.*

Copy the following consonants and write the name of each *in longhand*. Write twenty times:

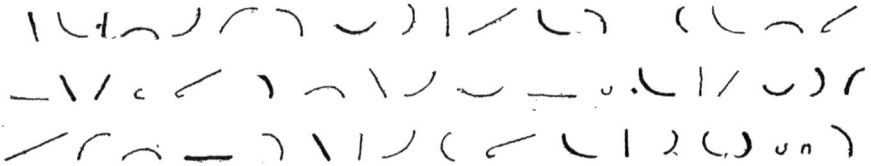

Write the shorthand characters named below, twelve times, *repeating their names* as you write:

Pee, Tee, Bee, Ess, Dee, Ish, Ith, Ray, Yay, Ing, Em, Gay, Lay, El, Hay, Kay, Jay, Vee, En, Ar, Bee, Zhee, Ef, Chay, Ray, Ith, Zee, Ef Thee, Pee, Gay, Ray, Ish, Zhee, Tee, Ing, Way, Chay, El, Yay, Zee.

LESSON II

Joining Consonants

ALL the consonants in a single word should be written *without lifting the pen* from the paper, the second stroke beginning where the first ends, and so on. The first perpendicular or slanting stroke of an outline should rest *on the line.* It will sometimes happen that the stroke farthest away will have to be read first, as in Tee-Jay. Seeing that both are written downward, one need never make a mistake in reading them. In writing Eff-En, Vee-Em and similar combinations, an angle should always be made between the strokes; but such combinations as Pee-En, Ef-Kay, El-Ess, etc., should have no angle, but rather *flow into each other.*

Consonants are written in the same direction when joined as when standing alone. *Heavy lines are never written upward.*

Write *ten times* the following outlines of joined consonants:

Ray-Gay, Em-Zee, Em-Chay, En-Ray, En-Em, Chay-Tee, Ef-En
El-Kay, Tee-Ef, Em-Kay, El-Ar, Ef-Kay, ·El-Ess, Pee-En, El-Ish
El-Pee, Ess-Kay, Em-Ar, Pee-Tee-Gay, Ray-El-Vee, Bee-Bee, Hay-En-
Dee, Em-El-Ar, En-Yay, Hay-Ing, Ess-Ing-Kay.

Copy the following exercise ın shorthand and then write it out in
longhand *ten times:*

REVIEW

1. What is the difference between El and Lay?
2. When should the angle be shown between joined letters?
3. In what direction are the heavy strokes written?
4. Where should the first perpendicular or slanting line rest?
5. When should the strokes flow into each other?
6. What size should the characters be made?
7. Name the characters that are written upward.
8. Which two letters have the greatest slant?

MOTTO OF THE WEEK

"There's place and means for every man alive."—*Shakespeare.*

LESSON NUMBER................................

LESSON NUMBER ....

LESSON NUMBER..

LESSON III

Dot and Dash Vowels

IN shorthand, there are *six long* and *six short vowels* represented by *dots and dashes*. The first six are called Lingual, because they are pronounced mainly by the tongue, and the other six are called Labial, because the lips are mainly used to produce them. These dots and dashes are divided into first, second and third place vowels, which occupy their distinctive positions at the side of the consonant; viz., at the beginning, the middle or the end. These positions are also numbered one, two and three, and are counted from the beginning of the stroke, thus:

The vowels have the same sounds as in the words written below, " ee " as in " we," " eh " as in " say," etc. The letter T is placed beside the vowels in this exercise merely to show the vowel positions:

ee	eh	ah	ĭ	ĕ	ă	aw	oh	oo	ŏ	ŭ	ŏŏ
we	say	pa	it	end	ask	awe	owe	too	on	up	foot

When a vowel is placed to the *right* of a stroke or *below* the horizontal letters, it is read *after* the consonant, and when placed to the *left* or *above* the horizontal letter, it is read *before* the consonant. Following are examples (write *ten times*):

pay ape jay age no own caw awk bay sham rain hope tall sap see

own eat age may say rope not hot nail hay dam rock sage cat bat

In writing an exercise, *read aloud* your letters and signs as you write them. After it is written, read it over and see whether you have properly applied the rules already laid down for joining consonants and placing vowels. After writing your shorthand, put the English aside and read from your shorthand notes. After a little experience, you will find them easy enough to decipher. Practice this frequently, until you can read correctly.

Write this exercise in longhand. (Key in Lesson V)·

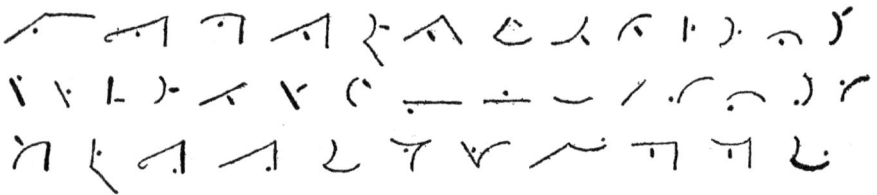

Write this in shorthand *ten times:*

Say, do, you, me, bat, he, she, knee, so, page, know, am, rat, aim, ray, pay, pig, name, hen, son, hay, hot, may, nay, root, thaw, law, note, raw, snow, ass, too, fear, at, pa, cat, ma, who, mail, saying, rope, sit, coat, wren, ran, doing, pail, said, run, cot, man, nail, come, ram, goat, dam, gun, shoot, hat, boot, tape, rock, made, range, money, honey, rain, rum, beer, cage, sage, range, owing, lame.

The following is a list of vowel word-signs which should be *committed to memory.* Write twenty times:

All already ought of or on two oh who to but should the a and

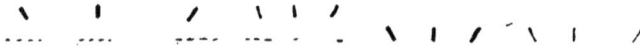

LESSON IV

Diphthongs or Double Vowels

THERE are *four* diphthongs or double vowels in shorthand, represented by small, angular signs. They are as follows (write
twelve times):

I Oi Ow Eu as in eyed toil bow cue Wi as in wife

The direction of these signs does not change, no matter what the
angle of the consonant. The sign "I" should always *open upward,*
"Oi" and "Ow" *downward* and "Eu" should open to *the right.*
When the junction is convenient, initial I may be joined to a following
consonant. The pronoun I may be joined to any following word by
one stroke, which may be written according to convenience. The sound
"Wi" as in "wife" is indicated by a small right angle. Write these
examples *ten* times:

I am, I do, I think, I will, wide, wine, wife

All first place, and long second place vowels, occurring between
letters, are written *after* the *first* consonant. All third place and short
second place vowels are written *before* the *second* consonant. Commit
this rule to memory. Write the following examples *twelve* times,
reading the words aloud as you write:

beam king tick tall doll mire make roam car bat idol rock rude

rope sop rag neck love house pipe ring rang money boiled poor

Write these sentences in shorthand *ten* times, using the sign words where *italicised:*

I will build *a* house *of* wood. *How* many years old are you? John wrote *two* letters *on* Monday. We should not *owe* money *to* others. *Who* put *all* this paper *on the* table? Have they gone *already?* *The* man knew they put oil *on the* water near *the* bow *of the* ship. Eggs should be boiled three minutes if you want them soft. My wife *and I* are going home at ten to-night. Send me *a* man *to* cut *the* hay. Don't bat *the* ball into *the* mire. See how thick *the* snow lies *on the* walk.

REVIEW

1. On which side of the consonant should a vowel be written to be read after the stroke?
2. Why are some vowels written light and others dark?
3. Where is a first place vowel written?
4. Where would you write a second place vowel after a horizontal stroke?
5. Where would you write a first place vowel preceding Ray?
6. Which diphthongs may be joined to the stroke that follows?
7. Where should first and long second place vowels, occurring between letters, be written?
8. Where should all third place and short second place vowels occurring between strokes, be written?

MOTTO OF THE WEEK

" When night hath set her silver lamp on high; then is the time for study."—*Bailey.*

LESSON NUMBER

LESSON NUMBER.................................

LESSON NUMBER......................................

LESSON NUMBER......................................

LESSON V

Uses of Ef, Vee, El, Lay

WHEN standing alone, L is *always written upward;* when joined to other strokes, it may be written either *upward or downward*, according to convenience. When written upward, it is called *Lay* and downward, *El*. *Lay* (upward) should be used when it is the only stroke consonant in the word, and for initial *L*, unless *El* (downward) would make an easier junction. *Lay* is usually written when it precedes a final vowel. Write this exercise *ten times:*

folly rely pull ball shall large people play doll only like long

After *Ef, Vee, Ray* and *Yay*, write *Lay* or *El* according as L is or is not followed by a vowel. After *En, Ing, Ish, Zhay* and *Iss-Kay,* use *El* whether a vowel follows or not. In all other cases, use *Lay*, whether a vowel follows or not.

Write in long hand, *six times:*

Write in shorthand *six times*, using word-signs where indicated:

Don't trouble other people; learn *to* rely chiefly *on* yourself. *The* lazy little man laid *the* long pole along *the* ground. Play ball, cried *the* people *on the* seats. It is folly *to* put large letters *on* small labels.

Please mail *the* bill *to* William Small, master *of the* school. *The* mail man pulled our bell *on* Monday night. Let *us* go away early *to*-night. Now, don't *be* lazy, John, but get *to* work. Jane, call *the* cat into *the* house. Don't drive *a* nail into that plank. *The* cow took *a* long drink from *the* pail.

Learn these word-signs thoroughly. Write at least *twelve times*, repeating aloud:

by, be, to be, each which much if for few ever have however see

so us thee they though hear are our why way away she shall usual

KEY OF SHORTHAND EXERCISE IN LESSON III

Rake, hate, made, wrote, soap, rope, John, show, low, day, say, may, saw, be, pay, do, so, row, bow, thaw, key, ache, know, each, eel, me, ass, ail, old, tape, had, rat, snow, nail, pail, ran, coat, note, sang.

LESSON VI

Uses of Ar and Ray

AFTER an initial vowel, use *Ar* (down stroke), except when the junction with the following consonant would be difficult. At the end of words (except after *En* or *Ith*) *Ray* (up stroke) is usually employed preceding a final vowel (as in row and fury); and it is used for *R* at the beginning of such words as *race* and *rear*, unless the second consonant is *Em* or some consonant that cannot be easily joined. Use *Ray* following an initial vowel, when *Ar* cannot be conveniently employed. In cases of two *Rs* at the end of a word, use Ray *doubled in length.*

Write this exercise *ten times:*

Ar-Em arch urge arrange earth rarer terror error aurora creek

Write in longhand *six times,* this exercise (Key in Lesson VII) ·

H may be expressed by the consonant sign or by a light dot or by a small tick, according to convenience. The *H* dot should be written by the side of the dot vowels and above the dash vowels, as shown below. Write *ten times:*

manhood loophole house hand head heap handy hope hall hang him

The dot should be read in connection with the vowel as: *He, Hay, Hah.* The *H* tick is written either to right and downward or to left and downward, according to convenience. Write this exercise *fifteen times:*

hazy ham hall hear hither holly hem hydra Hebrew hiss hence

Write the following sentences in shorthand *eight times:*

Let us hope *the* day will not be hazy. *The* rude man shook his head as *he* left *the* hall. *The* blind woman can hardly hear us here. Don't strain yourself by lifting heavy weights. Hickory nuts are usually very hard *to* crack. Plenty outdoor sport makes one healthy.

REVIEW

1. Would you use El or Lay in the word " life "?
2. When standing alone, which should be used, El or Lay?
3. How can you tell El and Lay apart?
4. Which form of L usually carries a final vowel?
5. When should Ray be used at the end of words?
6. Which form of R is usually used after an initial vowel?
7. When should Ar be used at the beginning of a word?
8. How many signs in shorthand expressing the letter H?

MOTTO OF THE WEEK

" There is unspeakable pleasure attending the life of a voluntary student."—*Goldsmith.*

LESSON NUMBER......................................

LESSON NUMBER................................

LESSON NUMBER

LESSON NUMBER...................................

LESSON VII

Uses of the Short Sign for Way

THE brief Way sign is joined at the beginning of consonant strokes as a hook to Lay, El, Ray, Em and En and at an angle to all other strokes. Write this exercise twelve times:

wail wore wine wedge week wet woke wave weighed acquire twain

The brief Way sign is used in the vowel places to indicate W combined with a vowel sound. The sign should be heavy for long vowels, and light for short ones. When Way is combined with dot vowels it should open to the right, and when combined with dash vowels, to the left. Write twelve times:

Wē Wā Wä   Wĭ Wĕ Wă   Wah Woh Woo   Wŏ Wŭ Wŏŏ

sweet watch walk wood railway sweep swine swing swelter swear

Write in longhand several times:

Write in shorthand eight times, using the Way sign:

Last week we walked seven miles in *the* wet. Which wheel did you say came off *the* wagon? What did you *do* when you went *to* Washington? Winter *will* soon *be* over *and the* wild flowers *here*. Some pigeons *have* white wings *and* breasts. *The* wanton shooting *of* birds is wicked.

Commit these word-signs to memory. Write fifteen times, repeating aloud as you write:

it at do had advantage common come give together think thank

was use will whole thing language (me my) (am may him)

The same sign applies to *me* and *my,* and next sign applies to *am, may* and *him.*

KEY TO EXERCISE IN LESSON VI

Arrayed in his Sunday suit, he ran away in terror. .The arch broke through an error of the builder. Leaning on his arm, she watched the aurora. Don't urge the animal too much. He is tired.

LESSON VIII

Uses of the Short Sign for Yay

THE brief sign Yay is used at the *beginning* of consonant strokes, but always at *an angle*. Write this exercise ten times:

yellow pale yoke yawn yore yam year yearling yarn yule

The Yay sign may also be written in vowel places giving the sound of Y and the vowel combined. Write ten times:

Yee Yeh Yah **Yĭ Yĕ Yă** **Yaw Yoh Yoo** **Yŏ Yŭ Yŏŏ**

year Yale yell yam your young youth unite yes yowl

Write in shorthand the following, copying the characters and speaking them aloud, six times:

Write in shorthand, eight times, using the Yay and Way signs:

The boys yelled *for* Yale. *The* young men took *the* yoke upon them-selves. *The* walls *of the* Union church were white *and* yellow. Yuletide comes *but* once *a* year. Did you say your name is Ulysses? *He* sailed *for* Yokohama, Wednesday *of* last *Week.*

REVIEW

1. How is the Way sign used to express the sound of Way combined with a vowel?
2. How is Way joined to a stroke?
3. Is Yay ever used as a hook?
4. How do you tell the difference between the Way and the Yay sign?
5. How do you tell the difference between short and long vowels?

MOTTO OF THE WEEK

" Blessed is he who has found his work; let him ask no other blessedness. He has a work, a life-purpose; he has found it and will follow it."—*Carlyle.*

LESSON NUMBER

LESSON NUMBER

LESSON NUMBER............................

LESSON NUMBER

LESSON IX

Iss and Ses

S AND Z, on account of their frequent occurrence, are represented by small circles, as well as by their outline strokes, the circles being more convenient for joining consonants. When written alone or joined to consonants not forming an angle, the circle should be made with a *left* motion (opposite to that of the hands of a clock). When S occurs between strokes, it is written in the position most convenient. The S circle at the beginning of a word is always read *first*, but *last* when at the end of a word. The vowels are read in their regular order, remembering, however, that an initial circle is always read *first* and a final circle always read *last*. Write these *ten* times:

S st sks srs hs sfs sls srs sms tsk psk msk nsm fsl nsld msls

lsl fsk up sup days fay face those blows chosen mall small nail

The sign for ss and sz as in faces, dresses, etc., is represented by a circle twice the size of the S circle, and the same rules apply to it as to the smaller circle. When a vowel comes between the two esses, as in system, the vowel may be written within the circle. Write *eight* times:

face faces pace paces nest necessity necessary tosses system

When a word begins or ends with a vowel, or where no other consonant occurs in a word, or where the first S is followed by a vowel, the s stroke should be used, as in easy, saw, used, says, size, etc. Write ten times:

sleep asleep puss pussy noise noisy Esmond assume saw says

Write in shorthand:

Always sup soup with *a* spoon. First-class stocks *and* bonds *are* considered good securities. Six *of the* students *are* pursuing *a* science course. Spring *is the* time *to* sow seed *if* you want summer flowers. *The* girls went shopping *and* purchased several new style dresses.

Write in longhand:

The following are word-signs. Learn them thoroughly. Write twelve times.

subject because several these this those themselves is-his

as-has hers ours ourselves myself himself impossible your

yourself yourselves influence he first any (know no) own

* Star means same sign applies to both words.

LESSON X

St and Str Loops

S T as in steam and test, is represented by a loop *half* the length of the consonant, and Str as in stream and mister, by a loop *two-thirds* the length of the consonant. Write *twelve* times:

steam stream must muster bust buster stack strike strife fist

The circle is added to final St or Str loop in the following manner. Write ten times:

masters busts busters fists tastes plasters fast faster last

Write following in longhand:

Write the following in shorthand four times, using joined sign-words where they occur, as indicated in italics·

The police hope that *for a* time *at* least *there will be* a decrease i
the number of burglaries on the West Side, because late last night *the*
succeeded *in* rounding up five men *who have* had *a* hand *. in the* jobs
The men were arraigned yesterday in *the* West Side court *and all o*
them were held. *Two of the* men were caught with *the* goods, whil
another *was* caught *by a* woman *who* held him until *the* policeman came

REVIEW

1. In what direction is Iss written?
2. Which is read first in a word beginning with a vowel, the circl
   or the vowel?
3. When written at the end of a word is Ess read before or after
   the vowel?
4. What is the difference between Ses and Iss?
5. In what direction is Ses written?
6. When should the stroke consonant be used for Ess?
7. On which side should the loop be written?

MOTTO OF THE WEEK

" There is an art of reading as well as an art of thinking, and an
art of writing."—*Isaac Disraeli.*

LESSON NUMBER................................

LESSON NUMBER......................................

LESSON NUMBER......................................

LESSON NUMBER

LESSON XI

The Initial Hooks

S you advance in your studies, you meet with various expedients for shortening the writing, in order to avoid putting down the longer forms of the consonants. You have already had the shortening by the use of the S circles, large and small. Next in order come the hooks, and the first to be considered are the initial hooks (at the beginning of a consonant) which add the sounds of L and R to the consonant. Thus, P becomes Pl and T, Tl, as the case may be.

A small hook at the beginning and on the *right* side of any consonant stroke (except M, N, Ing, S, Z, W, H, L, R), indicates that L is added to the consonant. Zhel and Shel have their L hooks at the *bottom* and are always written *upwards*. Write ten times·

pl fl chl kl thl shl tl pr tr chr kr fr thr shr mr nr

R added to any consonant (except S, Z, L, R, M, N, Ing, W, Y, H), is indicated by making the hook on the *left-hand side* of the consonant. Sher and Zher are always written *downward* and have their hooks *at the top*. When the R hook is added to M and N, the letters are made heavier. The L and R hooks may also be employed in uniting consonants, where the sound of R or L requires to be added, as in people, matter, fatal. A vowel written before a consonant with a hook should be read *first;* a vowel written after a consonant with a hook is read *last,* unless S follows, which is always final. Write *ten* times·

eater tree offer apple plea flea over civil saddle cycle close

Write in shorthand the following paragraph:

My *dear,* said *Mr.* Winter, you *should* learn *to care* for *other* *The young* medical doctor received his degree *from the* college. Ball playing develops *the* muscles *of the* body. Some girls are *very* skillfu *at* trimming hats *and* dressmaking. Let me *remark* that *the* old flint lock rifle, while good in its day, is now *a* back *number.*

New word-signs. Write *ten* times:

Principal able number truth dear during (which will) difficult

care from over (ever* very) either their other through (they will)

surely pleasure when one near manner while well wear where aware

* Star means same sign applies to both words.

LESSON XII

Iss Prefixed to Hooks

THE S circle is prefixed to a hook, as shown in the examples that follow. In the case of the R hook, Iss, Ses or St should be prefixed by writing the large or small circle or the loop on the R or *left side* of the letter. Iss or St written on the left-hand side carries R with it, as in strip, Str being read *first,* then the consonant; whereas stop is written St-P with the loop on the *right.*

Where a vowel occurs between the consonant and the hook, the vowel should be *struck through* the consonant, as in Portia, where it is written Pr-Sh with the O struck through the P; in bald the Aw is struck through the B; in Folsom, the O is struck through the F. Following the same rule, where the dominant vowel is a dot, instead of a dash, the vowel is *written as a small circle,* indicating that it is to be read *after* the consonant and *before* the hook, as in Charles, pail, chair etc. Write *ten* times:

sop sober spray stop strop said straw sister cider destroy

disaster scrape prosper execrable subscribe describe jasper

express sinner chair pail Charles tsk tskr sp spr psp pspr

chsp chspr stp stpr psk pskr ssp sspr ply supply mystery distress

Write in shorthand four times:

Do *be* careful, my *dear Mr.* Barker, *or the* child will fall. Well do I remember *the* case *of the* poor child *who* fell down *the* cistern.

Charlie, bring that letter back, it belongs *to Mr.* Smith. She sat in *her* little blue rocker greedily eating a dill pickle. I offered *the* child *an* apple, *but* she preferred *the* vinegar taste.

Write in longhand six times:

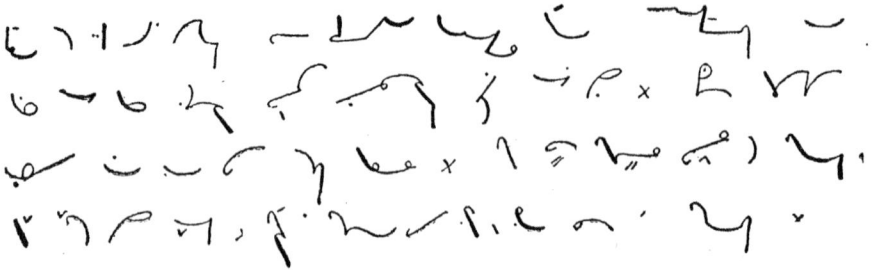

REVIEW

1. On which side is the L hook made?
2. When is it made at the bottom of a letter?
3. How do we know it is the L hook when it is written at the bottom of a letter?
4. How is the R hook added to M and N?
5. With what consonants is the R hook written on the right-hand side?
6. Explain how initial S is combined with the R hook.
7. Explain how initial S is combined with the L stroke.
8. Are the hooks ever employed between consonants?

MOTTO OF THE WEEK

" The art of a thing is, first its aim, and next its manner of accomplishment."—*C. N. Bovee.*

LESSON NUMBER......................................

LESSON NUMBER......................................

LESSON NUMBER....................................

LESSON NUMBER...................................

LESSON XIII

The Final Hooks

IN writing shorthand, you will occasionally make outlines which, although shorter, are not as easily read as the somewhat longer forms. As you progress you will become familiar with all forms, long and short; but it is a good rule to stick to the form which has the *greatest legibility.* In other words, shorthand ceases to be useful, unless you can read it readily and reliably. If you follow these studies closely, you will never fail to read your notes.

N and F are represented by final hooks, F being written on the *right* side of straight lines, and N on the *left.* The F hook when thickened, takes the sound of V. N may be added to any curved consonant by a small final hook on the *inside* of the curve. V is *never added to a curved letter.* A vowel written after a letter with a final hook, is read *before* the hook. Words with final vowels should be written with the last consonant long instead of shortened as a hook. Write ten times:

Ben Benny pen penny ton done rain rainy bone brain phone shone

line men thin son frown flown money profess terrify free fury

As you advance in your studies, you will find it practicable to omit many of the vowels and to write the words in the *first, second* or *third* vowel positions, viz., *above* the line, *on* the line and *through* the line. M in the first position would be me or my; in the second position it would be may, and in the third position Ma. S-Ing in the first position would be sing; in the third position, sung. Whenever you think that there will be any difficulty in reading, always use the vowel. Such words as tree, road, etc., can easily be read without vowelizing, as the context in most cases suggests the word.

Write in shorthand, six times:

Laying down his pen, *the* man told us *all* that happened that day. With *a* frown, Fanny glared at Ben *who* poked fun at bunny. Not being able *to* call, *on* account *of the* rainy day, Dan got Fred *on the* phone. John, please notify *the* tenant that his rent is long *over*due. *The* train ran around *the* curve at *a* high rate *of* speed.

New word-signs, learn thoroughly. Write twelve times:

before remembrance whatever truthful different done down

again careful gave generally even within then than men man

become capable opinion known capability disadvantage familiar

forever influential never investigation knowledge nevertheless

LESSON XIV

Final Hooks—Continued

S IS added to a final hook by writing a small circle *within the hook*, without lifting the pen. Never add a large circle or a loop to an F hook. S, SS or St may be added to the N hook by writing them in the place of the N hook. Observe the uniformity of this rule: you have already seen in the last lesson how the circle on the left-hand side adds R, as in stray; now with the N hook, when it is desired to add the final S, the N hook takes a circular form and is then written Ns as in tins, pins, cans, etc. In other words, the circle or loop made on the N side *carries N with it*. *Between* consonants, the circle represents only S. Write *ten* times:

proves scoffs strives chance runs cans residence danced buster

spinster spinsters ransom gainsaid destiny moons scenes

Write in shorthand, four times:

When dining, John dropped his spoon *which* bounced upon *the* floor. *The* dog pounced upon it, *but* after many cuffs *and* rebuffs, John gained it *and* punished *the* dog for *the* offense. Trains weighing tons passed *over the* culvert *which was* pronounced safe by scientific men. *The* prisoner offered no violence when summoned before *the* vigilance society.

Write in longhand, eight times:

REVIEW

1. Does the F hook ever have any other sound than F?
2. On which side is the N hook written?
3. Should words with final vowels be written with the N hook?
4. How is the N hook added to a curved sign?
5. Is the vowel read before or after the final hook?
6. How is s added to a final hook?
7. May a large circle or a loop be added to the F hook?
8. What form does the N hook take when S is added?
9. How is St added to an N hook?

MOTTO OF THE WEEK

" There are more men ennobled by study than by nature."—*Cicero.*

LESSON NUMBER

LESSON NUMBER..................................

LESSON NUMBER...................................

LESSON NUMBER................................

LESSON XV '

The Shon and Tiv Hooks

THERE are two *large* hooks called Shon and Tiv which we must next take up in their order. They are usually final, but not always, as these syllables sometimes occur in the middle of a word. Shon is always written on the *right side* of perpendicular and slanting consonants and on the *upper side* of horizontal letters. Tiv is written on the *left-hand side* of perpendicular and slanting consonants and on the *lower side* of the horizontal letters. On the curved consonants, Shon is written *within the curve*. Tiv is *never used with a curved* letter. Write twelve times:

passion operation intrusion provocation provocative operative '

nutrition edition vocative vocation fashions missions visionary

attractiveness activity occasion educational national destruction

DICTATION EXERCISE

In taking dictation, first copy out the exercise carefully in shorthand, so as to familiarize yourself with the characters. Then have some one to dictate *very slowly* the same dictation from the English, while you write it in shorthand. Then *read aloud* your notes to the dictator. You will find this slow work at first, but persevere and take the same dictation over and over again, at least *ten times* until you get the forms absolutely correct. *Don't try for speed,* but solely for correctness and legibility. Use the following for a dictation exercise:

ATHENS, N. Y., June 3, 1804.

The James Smith Belting Company,
    Buffalo, N. Y.

    GENTLEMEN: On August 2 we sent you our order No. 6791 for one 6-in. leather belt 18 ft. in length, your No. 563, to be shipped direct prepaid. We asked you to notify us on receipt of this order when you would make shipment, which we are anxious to have made as promptly as possible. We have as yet heard nothing from you.

    Will you please acknowledge this order at once, and state when shipment will be made, if indeed you have not already made it?

Yours very truly,
AMSDEN & GERRY.

    Write out the following in longhand several times (key in Lesson XVII):

LESSON XVI

The Eshon Hook

S·HON may also be added to a circle or loop by a small hook. It is then known as the *Eshon hook* and is the only one of its kind, so is easily remembered. Write ten times:

decision position transition administration musician vexation

opposition transitional compression equalization sensation

Write in longhand the following exercise:

Word-signs, learn thoroughly. Write twenty times·

objection subjection objective subjective acknowledge anything

irregular new now notwithstanding object peculiar probable refer

reference regular remarkable represent represented representation

representative something transgress whenever wherever highly

Write in shorthand, three times:

The Commissioner *of* Emigration took occasion *to* explain his position. *The* attractiveness *of* his vocation *was the* cause *of* his devotion *to* his work *to the* exclusion *of* recreation. *The* section hand *was the* plaintiff in *the* action against *the* railroad corporation. In spite *of* *the* opposition, *the* musician declared that his execution *was* exceptional.

Write in shorthand the following, several times:

Write *ten words* from the dictionary containing the *Shon* hook. Write *ten words* from the dictionary with *Tiv* coming between the consonants. Write *ten words* from the dictionary containing *Eshon* as final. Write *ten words* from the dictionary with *Shon* followed by a consonant.

REVIEW

1. On which side of a horizontal letter is Shon written?
2. On which side of a curved letter is Shon written?
3. Is Tiv ever joined to a curved letter?
4. Are the Shon and Tiv hooks always final?
5. Are circles and loops ever added to the Shon and Tiv hooks?

MOTTO OF THE WEEK

"Nothing great was ever achieved without enthusiasm."—*Emerson.*

LESSON NUMBER.............................

LESSON NUMBER..

LESSON NUMBER.................................

LESSON NUMBER......................................

LESSON XVII

Thickened and Double-Length Letters

EM is made *heavier* to indicate the addition of the sounds of P or B. This sign may take an N or Shon hook, but *no initial hook.* Write ten times:

swamp impostor humbug romp impose embezzle ambition lamp camp

Another labor-saving expedient is lengthening consonants. By doubling the length of Ing, ker or ger is added, but doubling any other curved stroke adds tr, dr or thr. Write ten times:

thinker hunger longer father mother older laughter thunder

floater anchored fielder slaughtered winter rendered water

The character Mp should be lengthened to express mpr or mbr.

Write in longhand eight times:

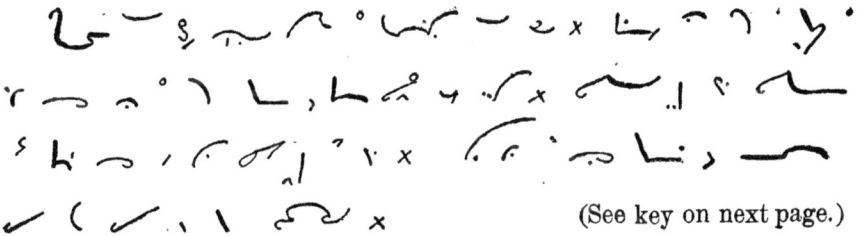

(See key on next page.)

Write this exercise out in shorthand carefully. Then write it *to dictation* in shorthand four times:

EAST ORANGE, N. J., June 17, 1905.

The Bengal Fire Ins. Co.,
      Easton, Pa.

GENTLEMEN: At the instance of several persons of consideration and influence, I am induced to make application for an agency of your company.

I have a real-estate office; and in connection with my labor in this direction I am led to believe that I can advance your interests, as well as my own, and also benefit this community by representing your well-known institution.

I am prepared to give satisfactory security and references, and request the favor of your early reply.

Yours very truly,
THOMAS REYNOLDS.

Write in shorthand, four times:

Father told Walter that by another winter, another hunter would wander over in yonder swamp. The scamp entered the room and blew out the lamp. He told him that he would get better shooting there and that the birds would be fatter later in the season.

KEY TO SHORTHAND EXERCISE ON PRECEDING PAGE

The drunkard, in spending the money, left his family in want. Taking the meat from the butcher, the old man made his way back to the damp house under the hill. Hunger had played havoc with the doomed man, who lay stretched out on the bed. The leader led the men back to the camp where they were to be court martialled.

DETROIT, MICH., April 16, 1907.

THE HAMILTON SHIRT CO.,
BOSTON, MASS.

Gentlemen: I understand you sell men's furnishings by mail. Have you anything that will show fully what you offer? I wish to buy but would like full information in regard to what I purchase, and also would like to know if I may return anything I don't like.

An early reply will oblige, Yours truly,

HARRY M. SAMSON.

LESSON XVIII

Halving to Add T or D

BY shortening consonants, either T or D is added. In the case of *M*, *N*, *L* or *R*, the letters are made thick or thin to indicate either T or D, as the case may be. Thus by halving, the word " add " becomes " added "; pot, potted; net, netted, etc. Vowels placed before the half length letters are read *first* and those placed after half length letters are read *after* the shortened letter, and *before* the added T or D. Final hooks are also read before the added T or D. Iss is always read *last*, no matter what precedes. Write eight times·

don't sent mind hand land band sand told made kind sold date

rapid fate vowed prayed played wind went stated replied contrived

ancient skate bold lived aimed seated deemed heart planned midst

drifts wisdom midnight lifted indeed rented factionists

In a few instances st may be written *upwards*, as in factionist and salvationist, to avoid changing the whole outline.

Write in shorthand, *six times:*

He leered at us as he mumbled, and his whole attitude was one of hate. The revolutionists fired on the fort; their bullets hitting pit-a-pat on its walls. Forty-five men were rounded up with the aid of the hounds. Seated on a stone bench, Pat aimed the rifle at the target, sending five rapid shots at the bull's eye. On the date mentioned, the students met and played their opponents, defeating them. Lumber being high, the builder contrived to make use of second-hand material.

New word-signs, *write twelve times:*

particular opportunity (till it) told (until it) (it will not)

toward (did not) don't (had not) gentlemen gentleman quite could

according cared cannot account good God that without astonish

establish (is it) (as it) used world heard might made somewhat

immediately put spirit rather matter

REVIEW

1. To what letters are P and B added by thickening?
2. What syllables are added by lengthening consonants?
3. What syllables are added to Ing when it is lengthened?
4. Why are some letters made half length?
5. Is the final T or D in a half length letter read before or after the initial hook?
6. Are final hooks read before or after the added T in a half length consonant?

MOTTO OF THE WEEK

" Work first, and then rest."—*Ruskin.*

LESSON NUMBER

LESSON NUMBER

LESSON NUMBER

LESSON NUMBER..

LESSON XIX

Ticks and Dots

"THE" is joined to a preceding or following word by a tick written upward or downward, like the slant of Pee or Chay. Write ten times:

for-the in-the which-the of-the to-the on-the but-the the-first

"A," "an," "or," "and" are joined to the preceding or following word by a horizontal or perpendicular tick, whichever may be most convenient. Write twelve times:

in-a is-a or-a but-a and-the and-a to-a of-a and-if-a

"On" and "should" are usually written *downward* when written alone, and *upward* when joined to other words.

A light dot immediately preceding a consonant stroke signifies "Con," or "Com," and a heavy one "Accom." Write twelve times ·

conscience committee convey construct accompany accommodate

community accomplish accompaniment companion comrade compel

At first you may not be able to recall some of the shorter forms of writing words, so do not hesitate to write them in the longer forms. Ease in the use of the shorter forms will come with practice. Besides, it is always better for beginners to use those forms they can *read most easily.* If you will *commit to memory every day, four of the short forms,* writing them, pronouncing them, and thinking them, you will soon be able to have them ready when the occasion demands. *Take frequent dictation.* Get some one to dictate letters to you, and to read slowly to you newspaper paragraphs. When you reach this point, take your note-book with you to some sermon or lecture, and take down as well as you can, complete sentences by the speaker. Of course, you will find at first that you cannot take more than a sentence here and there. Possibly you may be able to get two or three sentences together. By and by, you will be gratified to find how much you can take down. When you get home, write out your notes in longhand. If you have been careful, you will have very little difficulty in making out practically all of the shorthand.

Write out in longhand:

Write in shorthand:

Since the house was not large enough to accommodate the family the father made himself a committee of one, to arrange for the construction of a more commodious dwelling. After flagging the train, the accommodating conductor on the Connecticut road saw that we had comfortable seats. The Commercial Company's agent laid a complaint before the commanding officer, charging the absconding accountant and his accomplice with confiscating the cash of the Commercial Company.

Exercise for dictation. Write four times:

BROOKLYN, N. Y., Feb. 22, 1907.

MY DEAR MRS. TALLMAN: I have been notified that the taxes on your lot at Moriches have not been paid and the lot will be sold for taxes next week. I presume that for some reason the tax notices have not reached you and that you have overlooked the matter. If you wish, I will send my check for the amount—now $10.75, including some fines and fees—and you may remit to me at your convenience.

Please let me hear from you as soon as possible, as the time is short.

Yours very truly,

ALEXANDER ROBINSON.

LESSON XX

Dots and Ticks—Continued

A LIGHT dot after a letter signifies "Ing." This dot should be employed only as an affix, that is where it stands as a syllable by itself at the end of a word, as in sing-ing, ring-ing, walk-ing, hunt-ing, etc., but in such cases as ring, sing, king, wing, and fling, the outline consonant "ing" should be used. The affix Ing, followed by "the," is expressed by writing the "*the*" tick in the place of the "ing" dot. Ing followed by "a" or "an" is expressed by writing the "a" tick in the place of the Ing dot. Write *twelve times*:

doing flying running saying eating eating-a telling-the giving-a

sending-the leaving-the constructing-a following-the driving-a

Dictation exercise (*four times*):

DAYTON, O., February 27, 1897.

MCDERMOT PUBLISHING CO.,
SPRINGFIELD, OHIO.

Gentlemen: Kindly send us by Adams Express, at earliest possible date, the following books:

12 First Steps in Reading.
12 Junior Spellers.
18 Smith's Advanced Arithmetics.
24 Composition Story Books.

We thank you for your promptness in filling our former orders. Enclose bill at your very best rate, and oblige,

Yours very truly,

WALTER W. ROGERS, *Prin.*,

Union Public School, No. 6

Word-signs. Learn thoroughly. Write *sixteen* times:

mind (may not) not nature naturally under inorder acknowledge

afterward forward inconsistent indiscriminate indispensable

intelligence intelligent intelligible interest onward practicable

transcript understand understood important impose throughout

REVIEW

1. In what direction are the ticks for the and a made?
2. How is Con written and in what order is it read?
3. When should the Ing dot be used?
4. How are Ing-the and Ing-a written?
5. What does a heavy dot at the beginning of a stroke signify?
6. When should the consonant Ing be used?
7. How else may The be written than by a tick?

MOTTO OF THE WEEK

" Strike while the iron is hot."—*Scott.*

LESSON NUMBER.................................

LESSON NUMBER...................................

LESSON NUMBER

LESSON NUMBER

LESSON XXI

Prefixes

SIGN prefixes are designed to save time and labor of writing in full many words in common use, whose outlines would be difficult or tedious. In cases where the word may be difficult to read, or confused with some other word, write the outline in full. The following and subsequent lists must be *thoroughly learned by heart,* so that they can be read quickly and correctly. Write *twenty times*

Accommodate	Incomplete	Nonconducting
Circumstances	Introduce	Recommend
Conscience	Irreconcilable	Selfrespect
Contradict	Magnify	Uncontrolled
Decompose	Misconduct	Unrecognized
Foreknowledge	Noncommittal	

Explanation of prefixes in the above:

Accom. Dot at beginning.
Circum. Iss, written beside first stroke.
Con, Com, Cog. Light dot at beginning.
Contra, Contro, Counter. Tick at beginning.
Decom, Discom, Discon. Dee, written near word.
For-e. Ef, written near word.
Incon, Incom, Incog. En, above line or partly over word.
Inter, Intro. Net, in any position before word.
Irrecon. R, written near rest of word.
Magna, Magni. M, written over word.

Miscon, Miscom. M-Iss, written above word.
Noncom, Noncon. Nen, written over or through stroke.
Recon, Recom, Recog. Ray, written near word.
Self. Iss, written beside first stroke.
Uncon, Uncom. En, on line near word.
Unrecon, Unrecom, Unrecog. Ner, partly over word.

Write in shorthand carefully:

The International Congress recognized the incompatibility of discontinuing all warfare and introduced a resolution recommending partial disarmament. The magician contrived many interesting tricks which completely mystified his uncommonly large audience. Forearmed with self-respect and a clear conscience, the unrecognized man introduced himself to the constable, who had reckoned upon his being an accomplice. They recognized the fact that owing to the incompetency of the clerk, whose conduct was irreconcilable with good management, accommodations could not be had. Misconduct and incompetence, accompanied by circumstantial evidence, contrary to that incomprehensible statement made by the defense, compelled the judge to decide upon committal.

Dictation exercise (*four times*):

1674 UNION SQ., June 1, 1902.

MRS. JULIA D. BALDWIN,
    BABYLON, N. Y.

Dear Madam: In accordance with your request of May 15, we take pleasure in sending you our spring catalogue under separate cover, including a large variety of sample pieces of summer dress goods, representing all the latest and prettiest weaves.

We believe that we carry the largest line of high grade dress goods in this country, and the name " Johnson " is a synonym for excellence at a moderate price. If you will write us more in detail, we shall have the greatest pleasure in assisting you to make a suitable selection.

Trusting we may hear from you again in a short time,

Yours very truly,

MARTIN JOHNSON & CO.

LESSON XXII
Phrasing and Omitting Words

MANY of the sign-words in shorthand are arbitrary, but *all should be memorized.* This is very important, as you will find the sign-words of great convenience. A large part of your skill in shorthand depends upon the ready use of these short signs.

In writing briefly, it is permissible to omit " of " and " of the," and this omission is indicated by writing the words closer together as in " one of the men," " asked of him," etc. (see instances below). In all cases where numbers or dates occur, write in *plain figures.* This is a good rule to follow. In writing names, vowelize fully the *first* time as in " Brooklyn," " Washington," " London," etc. (see below). In repeating the same names or places, the vowel may be omitted.

In shorthand a period is indicated by a small cross, and a paragraph by two long parallel lines (see below). Where a shorthand character carries a capital letter at the beginning of the word, it should be indicated by *two small parallel lines* written under the word (see below). An interrogation point is made with the regular interrogation mark and a cross beneath it.

One of the men   asked of him   Brooklyn   Washington   London

Period Paragraph Interrogate Capitals as in Congress Charles.

In shorthand, you will find many phrases that may easily be joined without interfering with their legibility. By writing several words in this manner without lifting the pen, time is saved. Write ten times:

if you are   I am a   I am the man

I am in a   I was in a   in the mind of man

as well as   it cannot be   I think you will be

Write out the following exercise in full, in shorthand. Key appears in next lesson.

THE OLD OAKEN BUCKET

How dear to my heart are the scenes of my childhood,
    When fond recollection presents them to view!
The orchard, the meadow, the deep-tangled wild-wood,
    And every loved spot which my infancy knew;
The wide-spreading pond, and the mill that stood by it
    The bridge and the rock where the cataract fell,
The cot of my father, the dairy-house nigh it,
    And e'en the rude bucket that hung in the well!
The old oaken bucket, the iron-bound bucket,
    The moss-covered bucket that hung in the well.

That moss-covered vessel I hail as a treasure;
    For often, at noon, when returned from the field,
I found it the source of an exquisite pleasure,
    The purest and sweetest that nature can yield.
How ardent I seized it, with hands that were glowing,
    And quick to the white-pebbled bottom it fell,
Then soon, with the emblem of truth overflowing,
    And dripping with coolness, it rose from the well;
The old oaken bucket, the iron-bound bucket,
    The moss-covered bucket arose from the well.

How sweet from the green mossy brim to receive it
    As, poised on the curb, it inclined to my lips!
Not a full-blushing goblet could tempt me to leave it
    Though filled with the nectar which Jupiter sips.
And now, far removed from that loved situation,
    The tear of regret will intrusively swell,
As fancy reverts to my father's plantation,
    And sighs for the bucket which hangs in the well;
The old oaken bucket, the iron-bound bucket,
    The moss-covered bucket which hangs in the well.

LESSON NUMBER

LESSON NUMBER................................

LESSON NUMBER

LESSON NUMBER................................

LESSON XXIII

Affixes, or Syllables Added to Words

AFFIXES should not be used in cases where the words can be conveniently and quickly written with the consonants. The Sign-affixes given in this lesson should be carefully learned. A good plan is to write all the words you can think of in which they occur, repeating the exercise at least *twenty times.*

Ble, Bly—Bee joined when bel cannot be used. *Bleness, Fulness*—Small circle at end of word. *For*—Ef joined to word. *Ing*—Light dot at end of word. *Ingly*—Heavy tick direction of Pee or Chay. *Ings*—Heavy dot at end of word. *Lessness*—Large circle at end of word. *Lty, Rty*—Combined with any vowel following or preceding L or R may be added by detaching the final consonant from the group sign. *Ly*—By Lay written near end of word. *Mental, Mentality*—Ment near end of word. *Ology*—Jay joined or partially under word. *Self*—Iss joined, or when inconvenient, disjoined. *Selves*—Ses joined, or when inconvenient, disjoined. *Ship*—Ish written near or joined. *Someness*—Small circle at end of word. *Soever*—Iss-Vee joined.

List of words showing use of affixes. Learn thoroughly:

Profitable	Meetings	Manly	Themselves
Doubtfulness	Carelessness	Instrumental	Lordship
Therefore	Formality	Theology	Irksomeness
Dying	Instability	Zoology	Whensoever
Lovingly	Popularity	Myself	Whatsoever

THE OLD OAKEN BUCKET

Key in longhand in preceding lesson

LESSON XXIV

The Rain in Summer

Exercise to be written out in longhand and also copied in shorthand and utilized for dictation.

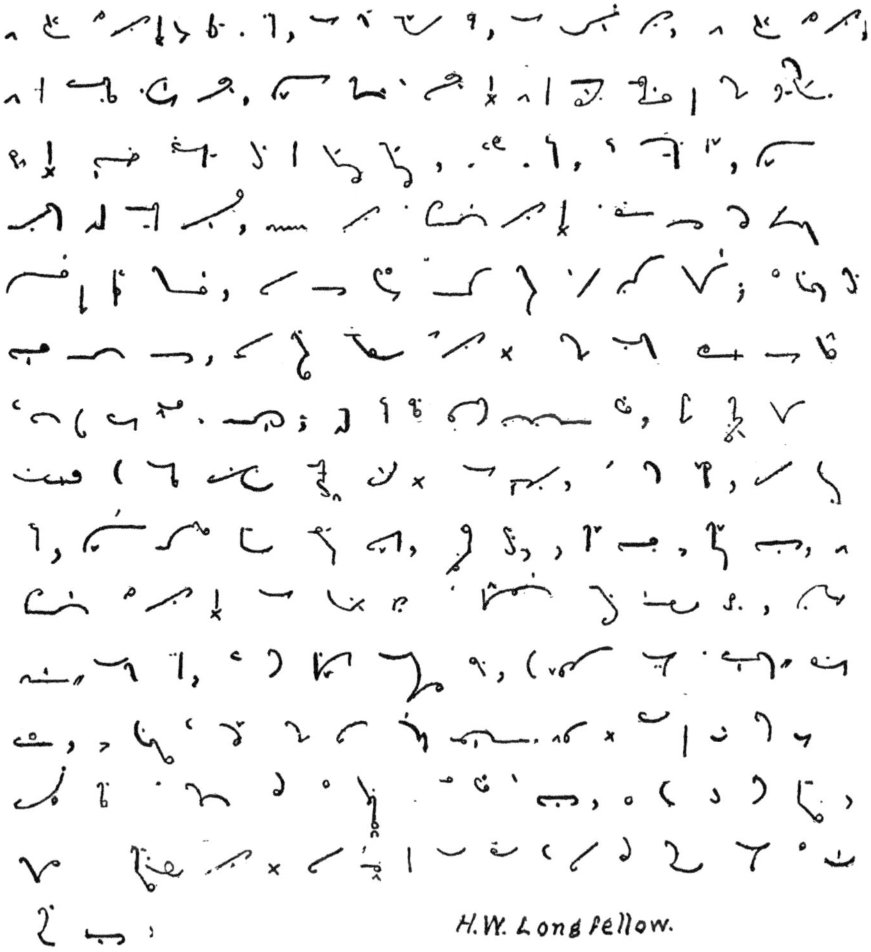

H.W. Longfellow.

TO THE STUDENT

A T the close of the Course, let us give a word of advice to the student as to future progress in shorthand. Do not be satisfied because you have become sufficiently familiar with the word-signs and abbreviations to take a good dictation. The motto of every student should be *Practice*, PRACTICE, PRACTICE! Procure a copy of " The Legend of Sleepy Hollow," in the Graham-Pitman system from A. J. Graham & Co., 1135 Broadway, New York City, 20 cents by mail. This gives the most approved forms of contractions, grammalogues, etc. The shorthand should be copied a paragraph at a time, to familiarize with the forms used; then transcribe into longhand.

TIME DICTATION FOR SPEED

Laying aside the book, have some one dictate to you from your long-hand copy. " Time dictation " for speed is a simple method and never fails to bring the desired result. Any printed matter will do—newspaper, editorial, news report, telegram, poem, or speech; write it out slowly and carefully in your best shorthand, using all the abbreviations you can. Then hand the printed matter over to some one to dictate to you, watch in hand. The first dictation should not be quicker than 30 or 40 words per minute. The same matter should be dictated four or five times at one sitting, gradually increasing the speed. Do not be hurried; rather resolve to make your characters clear and legible. Read your notes after each dictation, until you can read them as clearly as print.

At the next " time " sitting take a new exercise, following the same rule. Persist in this method, occasionally taking up old matter previously dictated. As you acquire ease in writing, the best forms and the clearest abbreviations will come more and more readily to your pen. Before long you will reach 100 words per minute. Beyond this point you are in the domain of rapid reporting. It only remains with yourself, by constant practice, to become as expert as could be desired. " Time dictation " is the Only Reliable Method of acquiring speed. Vary this with reporting speeches or sermons and taking testimony in court (questions and answers).

LESSON NUMBER

LESSON NUMBER............................

LESSON NUMBER................................

LESSON NUMBER................................

KEY TO EXERCISES

SHORTHAND FOR EXERCISE IN LESSON IV

KEY TO SHORTHAND EXERCISE IN LESSON V

Let us go away early to-night. Now don't be lazy, John, but get to work. Jane, call the cat into the house. The mail men pulled our bell on Monday night. The cow took a long drink from the pail. Don't drive the nail into the plank.

SHORTHAND FOR EXERCISE IN LESSON VII

SHORTHAND FOR EXERCISE IN LESSON VIII

SHORTHAND FOR EXERCISE IN LESSON IX

KEY TO SHORTHAND EXERCISE IN LESSON X

Strong men must eat plenty food to keep up their strength. The stone masons struck last week because they wanted more money. He learned under masters who taught him to make busts in plaster. The yellow automobile went past our house on Wednesday night. When the factory opened again, sixty men went back to work at their old places.

KEY TO EXERCISE IN LESSON XVI

The first edition of the morning paper has just been printed. We can't get possession of our property until the court has rendered its decision. The motion made, was that the education of the children be placed in the hands of the defendant. The plan of the administration met with no opposition. The administrative body declared the law was operative in various sections and that copies of the act were in the possession of the courts.

SHORTHAND FOR EXERCISE IN LESSON XIX

SHORTHAND FOR EXERCISE IN LESSON XXI

Printed in Great Britain
by Amazon